IN A VALLEY OF THIS RESTLESS MIND

HILARY DAVIES

In a Valley of This Restless Mind

London
ENITHARMON PRESS
1997

First published in 1997
by the Enitharmon Press
36 St George's Avenue
London N7 0HD

Distributed in Europe
by Password (Books) Ltd
23 New Mount Street
Manchester M4 4DE

Distributed in the USA and Canada
by Dufour Editions Inc.
PO Box 449, Chester Springs
Pennsylvania 19425, USA

ISBN 1 870612 97 3

Set in Bembo by Bryan Williamson, Frome
and printed in Great Britain by
The Cromwell Press, Broughton Gifford, Wiltshire

for Sebastian

and

for my parents

Acknowledgements

The author wishes to thank the Hawthornden Foundation for a
fellowship which allowed part of this volume to be written;
Dr Constant Mews, University of Monash, Australia, for his
encouragement and advice; Margaret Hebblethwaite and Father
Roderick Strange for their instruction and support.

The eponymous poem takes its title from the fourteenth-century
anonymous lyric, 'Quia Amore Langueo'.

Part of 'In a Valley of This Restless Mind' was published in *Acumen* 22.

Are the stunted oaks his gnarled guard
Or are their knarred limbs strong wih his sap?
. . . *Does the land wait the sleeping Lord*
Or is the wasted land that very Lord who sleeps?

David Jones, *The Sleeping Lord*

Contents

THE JACOBEAN MANSION

The Moment

That was the moment when, closing
The wicket gate behind me, I knew
That nothing would ever be the same again.
I knew I could wait before turning,
Very slowly, to look back:
An eternity to note precisely
How the falling sun would sketch
The branches, trace the millinery
Of the leaves. And then to turn
So slowly, looking backwards
At the glory of that·other life
Lived not knowing what would come,
Before the eye of the storm passing
Over our heads brings us the world's
Enormity, its frailness, driving
And driving the exquisite spike
Of ecstasy into our lives.

The Act

It's a slow terror settling;
The wind is full, the saplings
Hold up their new leaves, the sky's
A spring blue. And yet the thrum
Of this new melancholy chord
Sits in my ear: how can an act,
More fleeting, more luxuriant
Than air, move so to fear?
And all our efforts to hold on to it
As vain and pointless as this wind
Before me fretting a rose to and fro.
Here stalk the grey thoughts after ecstasy,
The burnt-out demoiselles of intemperance
Carrying mirrors where we find ourselves,
Not lovely, but with an unaccustomed
Famished look like harpies. Clouds
Grey and big with winter overwhelm the sky.

Charm for a Mortified Eye

Familiar eye that, when I open mine,
Finds me lying in the small hours' half-light,
And, as sleep shuts and opens,
Dresses me with love, so may I clothe
Your damaged sight with kisses,
Always wind and be wound
In this brief grace.

Faultlines

I should say that's how it was:
Catalogue the sweetness of it all, the measure
Greater than wine, the hurdy-gurdy,
Lovers darting across the street –

Say that's how it was. Our months
Turn already to years; we forget
How many cities we've lived in; the river banks
We've walked ravel backwards in the night,
Like lost highways.

That's how it was? Do you believe this,
My love? Your hands still grip mine
As if in the old way, as if in the old places;
Our words caress the world still
To take it in. Yet the levels we laid down
Are ribbed with faults; at night as we clasp
Each other – listen! – you can hear them grinding
Far underground.

By the Vézère

To you who were kind, I wish I had been more kind,
Though kind is what we were, for a time, friendly spirits
Flitting like dragonflies across a river, interlacing
Brother, sister wings. Like thunder, the clap of dies irae
Comes only after the event, bellowing back between the cliffs
When the boats are long asunder in the slow delta.

The Jacobean Mansion

This is how I wish to remember us:
In the garden of the Jacobean mansion
Watching the ball of heaven turn
Its treasures towards us like berries
And the cool night sweeping us
Up into its arms and all being benediction
Without knowledge of what wound
Would separate us, and both of us at peace.

STATIONS OF THE CROSS

I: *Christ is Condemned*

We are all condemned. We have all come
Out of the dark place, and will
Face righteous and false judges.
Behind them always stand the handmaids
Of retribution: our followers, friends.
We have all gone down in the night
On our knees and risen in the morning
To the silence of the irreparable.

Put out your hands; there's blood on them.
Open your mouth; there's gall on your tongue.
Now come into this room: look at its
Freezing walls, the niches where
Your private ghosts snigger or howl.
It's your own screams you hear.

II: *Christ Receives His Cross*

When, and how, we shall receive it
We do not know; for you, one November morning
With the fog ladening the beeches;
For her, a son wading into the tide;
And me, the nightly vagrancy of the blood.
How naturally our shoulders sag to accommodate
Our inheritance, each man instinctively shifting his weight
To find the position of least pain.

Once, in the back of the car, going eastwards,
I fell out of myself, out of time, out of even
Being human and looked on my parents' heads
As if they were monsters. How tenderly now
I remember the uneven shoulders, shifting
And shifting as under some unseen load.

III: *Christ Falls for the First Time*

The first time we think is the hardest
For we have never known what the particular taste
Of our own humiliation is. How could we know
The ground is so soft that we'll never be rid of it,
Always remember afterwards the smell of its oblivion?
No, we cry out on the lower slopes loudest,
Seeing around us the feet of what we imagine to be our tormentors.

Down so close, every stone's a mountain
Sliding its wall up to block out the sky;
We think, as we scrabble for handholds
On the scree face, that we shall come
Out of this valley, not seeing the ridges
Striding away to the end of the world like doom.

IV: *Christ Meets His Mother*

The first memory: sky like sheeted light
Slashing the avenue, the endless horizon
Towards which we are spun. You scoop me up
As the air spits and crackles with God's presence:
O protect me from his too hot embrace.
Down the eternal road you, holding me in your arms, run.

Now I steady your hand as you come towards me.
Ripping myself out of your body again
Would be easy baptism compared to this:
Making you unjoint the hoops of your mind
To allow this thought in, that our road
Together stops here, and my benediction,
Raising you over all women, fells you
Like the blow of an axe.

19

V: *Simon Helps Christ Carry the Cross*

I was looking over the wall, in the heat of the afternoon,
Listening to the silence of the burning road;
When around the corner came a crowd: of beggars,
Lepers, soldiers and pregnant women, talking low.
The dust from their sandals blotted out the sun.
Then it was that I felt thirsty,
And, seeing the fig trees full in my garden,
Reached and plucked, and bit into the flesh.

The rest came very fast. I fought, not wanting to go;
My own worries were plenty. They threw the fig fruit
Out of my hand and put there this staggering man's cross:
My fingers are stained, but with sap or blood?
Nights now are sleepless from my shoulder's pain;
No fig, no vinegar satisfies my thirst.

VI: *Veronica Wipes the Face of Christ*

Since childhood onwards, this fear of the sun.
A fear of what lay beyond city walls,
The desert cracking like thunder.
Starting awake with my tongue a tablet
Of salt, lips crusty as Dead Sea sand.
Keep under the walls, especially those encompassing
Orchards; cover, cover my head.

That's why, when I saw him come
In a pillar of dust over the hill,
He snared me: seeing the sweat like brine
Glisten his shoulders, hearing him rasp,
How could I not pull the veil from my hair,
And, wiping his eyes, comfort him?

VII: *Christ Falls for the Second Time*

What naïveté that all was! To imagine
There might have been some nobility in it!
How we do tell ourselves pretty stories
Even about our sins. More difficult now
Under a stinking noon, isn't it, and the smell
Of excrement in the air? We scrabble in wasteheaps
Outside the pale of the city, beginning to comprehend
How we packed the load which brings us down.

It's not our tormentors bother us,
But our inner fear and lies trailing us
Like a bird limed. Laughable now the pain
We thought others inflicted: sweet scourings
Measured against the degradation we sucked
Like honey time out of mind.

VIII: *Christ Addresses the Women of Jerusalem*

Cold comfort: our dugs shrivel at the news,
Wombs turn black as the tree blasted
By his tearless words. There will be dreams
Of bodies heaped along the roadside, flies
Loud in the sun; and sentries posted
With their crackling weapons
Along the staked-out limitations of our heart,
Our coralled, denying minds.

Yet there's compassion here: this flocking
Up the hill to accompany a death we all
Have known insistent in our thighs;
Our longing to atone for agony, to touch
With fingers that first held a child
The image of our own rack and exculpation.

IX: *Christ Falls for the Third Time*

Now it's as if he were already earth,
The master of the medium undergoing
This sudden haemorrhage of power underground.
This time the tongue is dumb; the other weepings
Seem now irrelevant, products of an earlier,
Rudimentary mind that begged for sanction,
Failing even the more obvious tests.
They were all children's baubles, in a dream.

No, here is silence. Be afraid. Afraid.
I said, afraid. Do you not see your parents
Hanging by their fingernails and their mouths open
Soundless? And now foresee yourself?
For here's the truth: this frailty is all
You'll have to beat against a night no man dares conceive of.

X: *Christ is Stripped of his Clothes*

Stripped of clothes, stripped bone bare,
Sheer bone bare, so naked even the inside
Of the skull is scoured for inspection;
But not the thoughts. So envious they,
Ah, orderlings, preparing the grave rites –
Who shall have the hemp, the sandals, all
Good men, good men, and don't smile
With your ironies; judgment will do you no good.

So search for purity; do you ask how? It's hubris,
My loved ones, to think rejection of these
Accoutrements, the dividing, the taking off,
Saves. Here's the regalia of nakedness,
The necessity for ritual: cleanse,
Purge, lose everything, face nothingness, yourself.

XI: *Christ is Nailed to the Cross*

What are we then, dog-men, faced with this? The maker
Here unmade upon his own creation devils
Our minds pinned on the road,
The leprous faces, the dust-veiled feet.
Like children frightened by the vampire's portrait
Or jaw-gaped mouth of the speaking dead
We dare only glances through our fingers sideways:
Shut them fast, quick! Cover over your face.

Turn left instead, here, for no man looks
A dying godhead in the eye. Here will do
For understanding what lies beyond our small mind's compass:
Small man, every man bellowing as the nails
Go through the bone. His screams echo round the hills.
Just at the edge of vision the soldiers tilt their cross upright.

XII: *Christ Dies upon the Cross*

We saw and desired him.
It was the picnickers, the squalling babes, the litter,
The warm stench of Sheol coming over on the breeze,
Which made us drowsy in that interminable watch.
A ragbag series of preoccupations keeps us
From entering the high stage with right bearing
And on cue. It's always muffed; we choose
The wrong key at the very holiest antechamber door.

The sound far down the valley roused us: first,
Like the lightest humming of bees startled by giants;
Then the boom of falling covenants, the shriek
Of new-yoked forms. It's these that teach us
We're now at the very heartland, under
The long crossed shadow of God showing how to die.

XIII: *Christ is Taken Down from the Cross*

Sit now in the cool house after catastrophe:
The men, in the low murmur of their lives,
Drink small and hastily the little clouds in the cup.
This afternoon's no different; always the need to shelter
From the furnace doors inching wider and wider
Off the bell of heaven. Copy the beetles:
They feel earlier than we the carapace crack
Under the jocked-up beams we imagine safe.

Black, black, the hooded matrons who have sometime
Opened their legs wide; this time going up the hill's
All their satisfaction. For this is the end
Of their couplings; ministration, not to the leap
Of the living, but to enter the violent embraces
Women suffer from dead sons.

XIV: *Christ is Laid in the Tomb*

Had paid gold for the hillside. Here
He had at last learnt to take pleasure walking
In the olive groves, above all, in the shadow
Of early evening as the day's fire whirled
Over the ridge. Had set up benches
For the sweet turning over of all his life
In his now autumnal mind. Brought daughters,
Grandchildren to remember him forever in this loved earth.

Under cover of darkness, now he runs ahead
Of the struggling women. He scrabbles back the stone.
Into this place for yourself intended translate
With shrunken, bloodied fingers its true occupant:
The sunken king, scorned merchant, traduced messenger;
Down the underworld walls the water hishes, victory, victory.

ELEGY FOR PETER HEBBLETHWAITE

Elegy for Peter Hebblethwaite

(for Margaret)

I

Six in the morning. All night through
The season's dead year cold has wrapped this cottage
In a crackling veil. The minutes inch
Towards the moment when to start will be too late
For me to keep our rendez-vous.
Mine alone the decision whether to stay or go;
The dangerous road unloops within my brain.
Then I recall that other dangerous road
I was excused when young, and failed to take,
And learned regret keeps faithful company
To actions left undone.

It's bitter cold. My steps are loud as thunder
Against the frost, the gravel and the walls.
This hour's a strange place, full of despair and brooding,
A world cave-black and shadowless, the very pit of souls.
I snap the headlights on. Just this small bit of lane,
The thought of getting in and out,
The mud, and bother for the care of gates,
To reach the narrow track along the hill,
Terrifies. Ease first gear in, gently release the brake.
The hiss of exploding ice beneath the wheels marks revolution.
This is the last journey I do for your sake.

II

So I remember a study,
And coming for the first time
Into your presence, Peter:
You were smoking a Woodbine.

In the cupboard plenty of whisky,
Your bearing slightly quizzical;
You opened your mind like a razor
To interrogate upon Pascal.

(Aroint, you existentialists!)
'I'm an atheist' I said
'Really?' the eyebrow flickered
'Then I must have misread

Some signs I thought I saw here';
The dialogue marched on
For weeks, for months. For years
I drank the schoolman's tone

Till I learned to comprehend –
And to comprehend's to love –
Your love of metaphysic,
Spirit and logic so to move

The mind beyond its manacles
That it begins to see
Its own falsehoods as madnesses
And then begins to see.

Still is that moment, Peter,
In memory's mould set fast,
Your bald head against the windowpane,
Your frame bulking out the past.

Still is the moment, Peter,
It hangs in the air,
Just one more time this morning
This sweetsome earth we share.

III

It's half-past eight; the car careers
Along a rill of crêtes and runnels,
Cwms, scree and glacial sweeps
Cross-hatched and crusted with frost work
That artisan angel, nature, casts in her cold forge,
Nightly, yearly, into eternity.
We think these beacons, hoping in the morning flare
To discover solace but these thin fires
Die instantly upon the moor
And are sucked down into the bog of death.

At Bwlch-y-groes the watershed:
Old saddleback of frontierland
Where the steep scarp warns vigilance
In the descent from this realm to the next.
I prize this place, anticipate
The bowl of softer hills, trout streams and shaded valleys,
The freely motoring in my loved marchland –
This all abolished: already by the shut inn,
The hand of dawn, like the pantocrator,
Signs across the sky the claw of God.
As I burst on the ridge, there is no land below.
Only the desert of a formless cloud,
While, angry and astonished, creation's primal eye
Fireballs across the fell.

I press the throttle, frightened, but more frightened still
Of coming late to our last rendez-vous.
You always were a wry one, never drove.
You had a way of lancing through a mind,
Then standing up, and showing us the door
As if to say 'I've done my bit.
If you've got bottle, you'll know what's to do,
Get on with it. Come back and show me
When it's in your hand'.
So I beat down my cowardice
And asked to camp in the hillfort of God.

I realise now (we're rising through the Cotswolds,
The sun's light shines like full moon through the fog)
It's always me returning to you: a myriad of roads
Criss-crossing up and down the nexus friendship
Since the first years spun on discourse and concord,
Affinities confirmed by those we loved,
Passed violently into contumely and interdict
Where we spent long years transforming silence, subterfuge,
Into a tighter fabric of trust, compassion, love.

And yet we must drop down
Down into the wasteland still
Where there is no line nor headmark
And the blindness brings us ill

The ranks of trees fly past us
But the juggernauts don't roar
Here danger is as stealthy as a mountaincat
Pacing on the limestone floor.

On and on past the lives flying
In a whiteout worse than the dark
This is the ancient Chaos
Where red entrails are the one mark

Of direction. All nature points the way –
The forests and the hedges and the blank ribbon breath
Of the frontier rivers and the freezing fog
Of the deadly motorway, all point: to Death.

IV

Twice I have wished to telephone you,
The first time, come at once, you said;
Your life hung in tatters on the wall,
Shocking and familiar as my own bed;
For there's no hierarchy in friendship,
When pupil and teacher are one,
When men howl, when women howl,
When innocence is fordone.

The second time, in a telephone booth:
The coins were in my hand, but I thought, no.
Instead drove home because it would have been
Too strange, too unexpected, just to burst in
And say, 'Last night I saw, after twenty years of labour,
The savour and the substance of what it is you do,
The gold of all the years of understanding rolling down
To other lives, the educator's river
That carries in its water the fertilities
Of everywhere it's been and lifts,
Like so many coracles from its banks,
The consciousnesses and the consciences
Of those who, unsuspecting, start on their own odyssey'.
I thought, no. Another time. You were already in your death throes.

V

The door bangs on the chapel wall
Dona eis requiem
For all the dead in the mourners' minds
Dona eis requiem
For father and mother and uncle and brother
Dona eis requiem
For those scarcely moved and those shuttered out of day by grief
Dona eis requiem
For the deceptive friend and the diffident enemy
Dona eis requiem
For old men who know much and babies who know nothing
Dona eis requiem
For betrayers, betrayed, the soft- and the hard-mouthed
Dona eis requiem
For your three children and your russet-haired wife
Dona eis requiem
For St Ignatius Loyola and your brothers in Christ
Dona eis requiem
From the bottomless pit, from the lion's jaws
Liberate them
From the day when heaven and earth shall open
Liberate them
From everlasting death on that great day
Liberate them
Liberate us
Liberate them
Liberate us

Bear all the coffins from the glittering halls
To the house where Lazarus lies
Where Mary and Martha groan in spirit
At the weary sacrifice
Where the dead come down from the streams and the hills
And up from the city sewers
From the high-rise block and the hospital ward
And throng our rooms of prayer:
Give them rest
Give us rest
Remember them
Remember us
Remember me
                    So be it.

VI

The freezing fog clamps the cemetery like a claw.
The sight's shut down, the ear's shut down,
The priest makes carvings in the bitter air.
I hold your letter, Peter; it came yesterday,
Signposting future travels of what you hope to say
Upon new plateaux of life's understandings,
Upon new instances of love.

But it's out of the cave of the dead
That you send this alive voice. How can we bear this?
When we place you so silent in the frozen ground,
You are not there. Then the invocations of the living
Are for balm to their wounds, since yours are extinguished;
Never again will you rage against love's hurts,
Nor cause them.
                                    Yet still we say why?
Why procreate to die?
Is this great question wrong eternally,
Should rather say: not to engender
Is to never be, for there can be no insight in the Void?
Here's the old rub: we do rise up and have the power
To foster love or hatred, bequeath atrocity
Or mere indifference, illuminate or blacken,
Become a thing of admiration or anathema.
This is our choice how to enact the world.

Guilt and responsibility remain forever
The wheeling broadsword in the hands of God.

VII

The cypresses spike the fog like sentinels;
Your wife's gold hair burns bright above your grave –
Peter, it's finished. You're sprinkled and set forth
Onto your different sea. Our forces ebb away
Down the long moment of the everyday
Into enquiries, jokes, a more manageable sadness.
The time of the living surges back: two hundred miles to go
And no let up on the dangers still to come.
Who knows how many years the journey takes?

31

On your last afternoon, you wrapped your dressing gown round
And rhythmed with your shallowing breath,
Maranatha, maranatha, O Lord, come.
I turn west. At Crug-y-bar night falls.
Mile after mile I probe into the dark,
Meet just the lights of other travellers
That wink but offer no mark of help or recognition.
The car draws near the hill
And never can one revolution of these wheels
Turn back. In your dying, Peter,
You teach me this one last thing:
We have a whole lifetime, but not a moment more
To drive our road. Make haste, therefore,
Make haste, to find the key to our own city
Before we reach the gates
For there'll be no answers given
Once God has clanged the door.
You said, 'The philosophical treatise is complete';
Peter, remember me when we next meet.

I'm home. Love awaits inside. Lights off.
Over the countryside, no sound. As I go in,
The hiss of exploding ice beneath my feet
Says: revolved time.

WHEN THE ANIMALS CAME

France

Valley of the Vézère

Upper Paleolithic

I

Autumn

When do the animals come?

After the great heat and the midge time
On the rivers are done. In the season
When the air's no longer dense with the thrum of insects
Or tern cry, the metamorphosis comes.
Each one of us locates it differently – a speckling on the leaves
Whirled from the birches, the ripening of the dark rowanberries,
The grilse quickening to come up river,
The steppe bursting open like a fruit underfoot.

                                   We know then come the mists,
Weeklong exhaled like fire from the summer river,
A burning, consuming assumption of water into the air,
And the forest is hung with green glass.
This is the still time, the time when between heat and moisture
The trees seem to strain to a voice we don't hear,
The leaves all taut as if strung on a bow.
We lie exhausted in the nervous woodland,
Waiting the first mark of change,
The slow uncurling of an aspen leaf that bellows
In seconds to stormwind, baying and snapping
The tree crowns before it as reindeer go down before wolves.
We know fear then, nor cower never so close to the earth
But the sky spits phosphorescence, and the horizons
Boom like a thousand precipices exploding from the cliffs.
The night rains sweep in cold air;
The forest settles.

                    It's then that the animals come.

      ★   ★   ★   ★   ★

How do the animals come?

                          I'll tell you how I saw it as a youth –
My first hunt, so stationed with my father
Along the river bed, and told to watch.
The reconnaissance parties of the younger men
Sleep on the plain, hard to the elements,
Turning their faces, all day, all night long
Eastwards, licking the wind for the first signs of ice.
In the dark, you can hear them chanting, laughing
To chase the apprehension from their hearts;
Below, the tribe refines and overhauls equipment:
Burins, scalpels, missile projectors; the clack, clack,
Clack of stone on stone and sound of many voices
Rising from the autumnal foliage up to the watchmen on the rocks.
Make the channel here, the funnel guiding down
The gully to the fording place, cut back the branches,
Let the treacherous light through
To where the enticing water glitters and leads down.
Make sure this way they come.

Still full of sleep and early morning,
The kinsmen cooking, mothers picking lice,
When the frightened mouths yell down the rockface
'Now!' I take my station by the river trees
And watch the men come out. All hard hunters,
The tight-sinewed and the massive-muscular,
Those who cunningly tell the places, even though pot-bellied,
The hungriest, most recently admitted, with their javelin arm
Too hastily flung back. Greased and dressed towards their labours
They picket stealthily along the stream and prime their weapons.
The dew falls in their hair.
Birds chirrup, then sit, still; we hear a rustling
Where the women corral their children towards the shelters
And turn their chattering in upon the rock.
The strangest of all silences fell then; though nothing
In the crack and spit of things, the leaves' whisper
Or faint catching of the tide upon the gravelbanks
Was altered, it was as if the very tension
Of those minds placed there raised up a presence
From the valley floor who, gigantesque, passed from us
Between the fir trees and, with one gesture of his massive hand,
Threw down the die of fate.

Now the air cracks: the far boom of hooves
Unrolling forwards is like the striding of a tidal wave
Out from where continents shock.
Thus the army of desire for south, for west,
For warmth, approaches, and we step to meet it.

Interminably long. The river starts to sizzle.
At last the leader treads with caution over the cliff scree
And down; we hear the scratch of fetlocks as the deer dig in
To slow the drop. Their heat's upon us;
We can feel their breath. The young keep close
Beneath their mothers' bellies; the bulls ride, wary, pendulous,
Along the edges of the trail. And still the mother of the herd,
Who knows the landscape and the destination,
Glides them down the mudpath to the healing water.
Among the trees hands sweat upon the javelins.
And still the wily female guides, and fails,
And leads them to their death.

We go for the young, much easier to kill.
How they scream! How much they want to live!
Their tongues twist purple round their muzzles,
Their mothers roar a roar you never heard.
Thus we turn them under the water with harpoon,
Assegai, hourlong; the soft river
Slips away with their soft blood.

    ★   ★   ★   ★   ★

The hunt is finished. Till a late figure
Descends, snorting, through the aspen wood –
An old bull, setting us a prize – we jostle
For position as he hesitates, perturbed and anxious,
Flaring danger at the water's edge;
The warriors also, each stepping now the camp fire dance
Of animal and sorcerer for real.
But desire must outstalk fear: the bull must go
South with his females to the grazing lands;
The young, the glory-hungry hunters show themselves.
He crashes forward in an arc of sunlit water,
Emerging from a maze of falling gold
To bid for life. Across the flat, smooth rocks
One man snaps out, his eyes upon the furling dewlap –

The prize! the prize! – wrongfoots his dance,
And falls among the tides. Beneath the hooves,
The massive withers, he's rolled and pounded round the current,
His jaw and breastbone sifted to the sea.

II

Winter

Winter. Deep snow upon the overhangs.
You can hear the limestone cracking far above
Where ice beds down in fissures
And snaps his unpredictable axe.
I've seen whole rockfaces jump from their roots
And make a bloody mockery of the families beneath.
But still we live here.
The hollow's round like shoulders
Squared against the steppe winds that will shred
Your face and body like a knife.
                                        Listen.
All around it holds and passes to us
Our minutest sound – a sigh, the rustling
Of a chilblained leg beneath the pelts,
Sinhikole whispering to his wife as they embrace.
Here is the arena of human life.

Look. Lean over. Can you see
The paraphernalia of morning cares
Transforming loneliness? How all the families
Are busy in the everyday of coming again live
Into the world and recomposing it?
Our tribe, eases; the scent of its breathing
Catches on the fires. Each family has a preference
For a different wood – the heady juniper,
The magic silver curl of birch, or querulous tremor
Of the aspen twigs shivering like waterboatmen
Even as they separate us from death. For victory
Over death at night's understood in all the smallest
Of these celebrations. The women choose
Among the herbs they'll wrap the crackling reindeer in.
The men chew pemmican or hail friends across the gully.
A ptarmigan shrieks upwards in the wood.

Sinhikole's daughter, two years old, startled,
Lifts her gaze along the treetops and is lost in air.
Nearby her mother checks around her
For all the utensils necessary to begin her work.

★   ★   ★   ★   ★

What kind of industry? The art of judging stones.
Come into the workshop. Sit here. Take one of these.
Feel how the nodule fits into your palm,
How its thin sheath of white mimics work-worn skin,
That subtle graininess. Here, as it is, an object of little matter,
An unexplained, unself-revealing thing
Of arbitrary shape and size, a toy for children
To toss and marvel at when every time
It lands into a different figuration in the dust,
But nothing more.
                    How our intelligences do lie to us!
How they love to slide across the surface,
Never snag themselves upon the cunning razors
Of what lies within. Let us release it. Angle it right.
Test it. Test gently. Tap again. Now strike!
Forcing won't do: all around lie the bits and pieces
That betray a want of adequate thought
About the essence of the stone inside.
Yet when you get it right, flake slips from core
Like fur from flesh: you have your means of living
– The carving up of horse and bison, hide cleaning
For your shoes, clothes, shelter, the preparation of the wood
For kindling, fish hook and spear head.
Now you have witnessed the opening of the mystery,
Do you understand how thought itself waits
To leap from the stone? The moment when,
Beneath your fingers, the silica emerges as your mind projected
And prehensile on the outward world, not just for living,
But emblematic of a lifetime's wrestle
To enact the miracle of making other,
The flint flowering from your imagination into laurel leaf?

Sinhikole's wife smiles, selects, with casually expert eye,
A gleaming nodule from the workshop floor.
Begins again. In the canopy above, the birds chatter, uncomprehendingly.

III

Sinhikole and Ezpela

'Ezpela, do you remember the first meeting,
How we had come into the hills
To take part in the season's ceremonies,
And it was warm and in the evening?
I heard you by the river bank, laughing,
– Water incandescent like a comet in the air –
And you were turning and turning in runnels
Of lightning down back and breasts
As you smoothed your way through the eddies,
And the reeds caught in your hair.
The sun turned then to a still, slow ember,
Subtending the whole of nature through your frame.
And it seemed there, under the leaning willow,
That your belly was dappled with roan and silver,
And down your thighs shifted the powerful muscles
Of salmon coming home from the sea.'

'The first night we were alone –
The marriage tent, the guttering lamps, juniper scenting the room –
You came before me, took off your belt, deerskin, shoes,
And knelt naked; the ivory and amber of your necklace
Like pebbles glossy in summer pools.
And I desired you.
To touch your shoulders, neck, breast, thigh,
Full sex, was like a leap into a land
Where spirits counterpoise, our coupling
A confluence of waters where the tides of reciprocity
Meet and roll. Upon this understanding,
Life spins: man's entry into woman,
Woman's rejoicing in the sex of man,
Are not the conjuring of an hour, the body's stratagem
For breeding or some assuaging of a jiggle in the loins,
Unless we fail to comprehend how in this act
We make of ourselves a new thing, richer than before,
A source that ever, as we drink of it,
Wells from underground.

So many years since we lay by that fireside
– You kiss my slack breasts, I stroke your lined face –

40

Are like these cliffs shaped by the caressing river,
Particular, known in every recess, fond.
I take your sex in my hand; open my thighs.
Let us invent ourselves once more.'

IV

Spring

A cry. Thin, the cry of a new-born
Beyond the tepee. Sinhikole's wife wakens with a start,
Throws back the flap and catches tight her breath
At how the world has shifted overnight outside.
Her daughter runs, head-high in grasses,
After the image of a crimson butterfly.
Across the river, a faint, new blush
Of saxifrage and dandelion – red, citrus, blue –
Trickles down cliff and through the meadows like the meltwater
You can hear splashing in the rock pools out of sight.
And strewn along the riverbank's the necklace
Of the newcomers' tents, laced like different ambers
On a chieftain's rings or spiders' webs in dew.
This is the season of the many dialects:
They lift like swarms of insects, fastening upon the riches
Of the feasting here, the intermingling of hearts and pollen
That changes from seed to nectar to life.

My daughter, come to me: we'll run down
Through these spring flowers with you upon my shoulders
To where you'll play these hours long
Among the bushes and in the water's shade
With your new comrades. How you do look like elvers,
Slippery and supple, insouciant as the dace is of the pike.

        *   *   *   *   *

Stand close to the edge.

                      Two hundred feet above the river plain
Is by far the best location to judge the extent
And enormity of what happens here.
From all sides and the limits of your gaze

41

You see the subtle movements through the trees,
The slow cortège of tribe and subtribe with their accoutrements
And baggage arriving through spring mist and smoke?
I number them all, yearly, the minute differences
Of lilt and custom: these, crawling under the vast overhangs
Of our eastern tributaries, come from upriver
On the snow-capped plateaux from where the teeming sources
That demarcate our world foam down.
The file that comes from westward always brings
Tales of a great delta; there, in a thick and viscous tide,
Our river, black, unrecognisable, winds to its death
In salt and the bitter cry of malevolent birds.
Here are our sisters back from every tiny gully within a day's walk,
Married into new fraternities, escorting husbands,
Or our cousins showing the various tattoos of bird or fox or insect
That mark them for ever into another chain.
Another chain – for this is why we meet here,
What makes our privilege of living between cliff and river
Matter is this point of pilgrimage, the precise organisation
That makes possible the necessity of praise.
This place is the omphalos of what we are.

*   *   *   *   *

'Omphalos is hard. Menacing. Dark.
Make sure your torch is primed, the wick in your lamp
And suet in it. Follow on your belly through the passageways
And count every stage of deepening terror as a kind of grace.'
Sinhikole, cold from years of teaching, exhortation,
Squats mechanically at the chamber door
And does the gestures. Puts on the birdmask,
Smears chest and cock with ochre, presents each initiate
With the necessities for such a journey; they smell
The unaccustomed objects, try them on their palm.
Already thirst, anticipation, hunger begin to bite.

Inside, it's cool, the sunglare still falling from the outer hall
Turns all to moonlight, hangs it with a veil
Of unfamiliarity: the walls are oyster shells
Or women dancing; the roots of pearly, unnatural trees
Frond down from the roof.
Look your fill while the light still holds –
This is the antechamber of dread.

*   *   *   *   *

Cold, damp, like dead men's hands running
Along your back and shoulders, between your thighs,
And then this sight – or rather, no-sight, what you've never seen,
No night like this has ever blindfolded stars, put out the moon;
Always we receive the phantom, shadow, to lend us body
In the absence of our noonday selves.
                                        Not here.
Here is no sense of up nor down, nor time nor season;
No colour, no form with meaning, no warmth,
No sound, no breath of air, but black invading every orifice,
Black in your ears and eyes, black on your tongue,
Black behind, above, beneath, black to annihilate thought,
Black to drive out the world, black to usher in insanity.

        *   *   *   *   *

Lift your torch and run it along the gallery wall.
This is what you have come, and now must learn, to see,
Bereft of all the things you use to define yourself outside.
Here you have nothing but what lies within your field of vision,
Buried in the very viscera of earth.
No-one knows when we first found a distance
Between the felt reality of bark, or pebble, or muzzle
And a reality within the mind – call it the inability
Not to recall, to put out of our mind the presence
Of what we cannot see. Don't think a few visits here
Will make of you an adept; remember always
You will never know except by exploration and re-exploration
What it is you seek. All those who have finally achieved
Some wisdom in these caves know this means hardship, separation,
Hours in the flickering gloom just keeping watch.
Fix upon one feature: the sprung ears and head
Of this red stallion, the way he leaps towards his mare,
Or the moult line here upon the bison, the irritated gait of rut.
Sit very still before these images
And soon this enclosed space and visionary drink
Work their effect. Do you feel how the cave imperceptibly,
Relentlessly, fills with movement, and the clayey stink of tomb
Is overlaid with musk and grassy breath?
And somewhere from the uterus of time,
From the passageways which lead off down from us,
Rises the rumour of a bayed rhinoceros –

Out of the shadows he starts, sniffing the air,
Scenting us, as quick as a chamois sheering away on his toes
And gone. Swimming in an alchemical river,
The herds of stags sprout antler forests reaching up to heaven.
Above them, a one-ton aurochs gyrates gently in the air.
Behind the calcite curtain, one hundred thousand lions
Prepare with loping strides their sortie from the stone
And jut their eager heads along the eaves.
Their baby mammoth prey floats like thistledown on the breeze.
Do you hear now the thrumming in your temples
That is the attunement to these metamorphoses,
The preparation for the most difficult place?

Come to the edge; you must hang in the void
Before you can climb down towards the last degree
Of the transfigured world. The draught that lifts your hair
Is the breath of earth herself.
There is the sacred wall and wound that all who come here face.
Man, bison, meet – but not the grazing animal,
Nor the elder squatting by the fire; no, here they're wound
Upon the spit of where we come from,
Pierced by the spear of what futurity,
They are the means whereby we enter and pass out of
The act of time and its responsibility.
We think of time as the turning of the seasons,
How we wait each year for the inexplicable cornucopia
Of beasts and plants that bring our lives grace,
And how at night and in the relations of our genealogies
We honour them. We call ourselves 'bull tribe' –
Our brotherhoods, 'bear', 'mammoth', 'aurochs', 'horse' –
Each seeks an explanation for its particularity
In the repeated interrogatory and celebration of these forms.
You've seen the sum of all the wisdoms of these observations
Vault and jubilate and shimmer in these caves.

                              Down here is otherwise.
No monument but a frozen image
Of dying man and disembowelled bull
Who are the illumination of the other side of time.
Here is the fierceness of the pointed moment,
The moment when it is no longer possible to play
Among an infinity of possibilities, or stay the change

Of harpoon strike, horn-gore, the passing of what is seen
And present into the unseen, the perpetual elsewhere.
All bulls are contained here in the tilt of the head,
Horripilated mane, the entrails hanging like a sex between the legs,
And all men in the birdman, privileged of the tribe,
Who must, in order to make bearable to us
The horror of our journey out of time,
Suffer the wound, suffer the exiling moment,
Be powerful enough to take upon himself
The burden of fear, of loss of strength, disgrace,
Extinction, that we have come, in the pit of these dark caverns,
To encounter and defy.
                    For no-one who has not suffered wounding
Hopes to heal.

        ★   ★   ★   ★   ★

The light and noise of the upper world hit them like an axe.
How suddenly the very soil seems sinewy, the trees roar unbearably with
      life!
They stagger with the newfound weight of living,
The chaos and the prodigality of what seemed routine:
How will they touch their wives at evening?
Or bear to look at the tender limbs and bodies of their children,
Towering like gods around the fire?
Sinhikole shades his eyes, steadies himself
To retain a moment longer the certainty
Of the caves, the double hinge of two realities
Upon which man's spirit sings.

How sweet he is able now to think his wife's voice calling . . .
A wrong note. Too many voices. Shrill.
Sinhikole starts from his reverie to see a line of women
Scrambling up the rocks.
                    Dignified, his wife comes before him,
Tells how, while he was journeying in the cavern,
His daughter, after bathing in the river,
Complained of headache, fell into convulsions,
And, as dawn broke, in agony, died.

They go down together to the encampment.
Sinhikole's birdmask trembles in his hand.

V

Summer

'Deep noon. Canicular in the trees.
A kind of stealth about the swelling green,
A fattening along the waterways
That overhangs and darkens the place.
When we walk the trails, a carapace of leaves
Shuts round us, and a quarantine of sound –
Not of sound absolutely, but of the sounds
With which we came here, and which walk
In our blood. We do not care even to sit and learn
The unfamiliar cadences – a coat of fear
Rustles everywhere, worst in the windless forest
When, unseen, suddenly, a boar crashes breathily away
And all the undergrowth shakes with demons.
Look at the ground. These leaves in millions
Patterning themselves into the soil become a veil
For knowledge: I came this path yesterday
And could not choose which way to go.
If you look up towards our shelters,
The foliage moves to meet you like a mob of bees.
Did a precise summer bring us this change?
Or was it over many ages we failed to notice
The dwindling of the reindeer, their coming later,
Ever later, and stories from our brothers far down in the delta
Of tides that do not recede? The plains where our men
Watched, and listened for the hooves, are sunk themselves
Beneath a wash of trees; our hunters grow
More furtive in the forest, spend ever longer
Away from the encampments, and, when they do return,
Sit separately in huddles with their wives,
Glancing towards us, as if to speak of secrets,
Unfamiliar herbs and animals, a different way of tribes.
The initiates still come, though fewer –
The forest is a savage place, and some have starved
At its very core – but no more do we visit all the sanctuaries.
For long ago we found it ever harder to crawl amongst the massive roots
That gagged the entrances, or tell a man's trace
To the sacred caves from the trails of roe-deer in the tanglewood.
And ever harder to elucidate the histories

46

When the going of the animals sealed off our understanding of the past.
The old cannot go after them; and those who choose
To hunt into unseen territory have lost the very contours
Which made the message real.'

                                         Sinhikole touches his wife's hand.
High on the upper levels of the cliffs he leans
Against the limestone, warm from the setting sun,
And studies the outlines of the plateaux
Across which the brotherhoods used to come.
The river runs a curl of silver through the trees.

The bulls leap in the sleepless sanctuaries.

The silence of the forest grows apace.

IN A VALLEY OF THIS RESTLESS MIND

I

Héloise, Abbess of the Convent of the Paraclete

The wood dove's murmur drives us mad
With memories: in this place where nothing
Under noonday moves, the simple flight of flies
Could be the city's bellow, the great grey river
Flushing all before it through philosophic streets
Of horse, oxen, merchants, clerks, humanity's high tide
Swilling its quiddities against heaven's gate.

Heaven's gate: cathedra rising from the fluxing water
And crowded round with habitation, lesser excrescences
Of its own spiritual life, noisy porticoes, markets,
Disputations, the rustling friendly robes of nurse and guardian.
The lines of sunlight draw their trigonometries
Around the still point of the city, veritable chair
And ship upon the waters, centre where I learnt reason first.

II

Bernard, Abbot of Clairvaux

Reason out of Brittany? You must be joking.
Basse-Bretagne? The men there risk heretical foodstuffs
And the women worse. Don't touch them.
It's lichen, endless rain, strange outcrops
On the sandy levels not put there by God.
Brittany's reason is an insane aberration
Loud in the rest of the land. Expect not thought
You could call orthodox.

III

Peter Abelard in the Place of his Birth, Le Pallet, Basse-Bretagne

How shall I get preferment in this God-forsaken place?
An outlet for my mind, my talents that here have nothing
But the stupid ox and stupid villager upon which to exercise themselves?
The roll in the land is wonderful, yes, the corn, the kitchen gardens,
But no sense of anything other than the rut of preoccupation
With the interminable cycle of the everyday prevails here.
Is there a kind of slothfulness of mind that indicates
A marking off from God? How can we trust ourselves
To know things unless we labour from every niche and corner
Of our intellects to flush out obfuscation, old wives' tales,
And attempt to square perception with our true beliefs?
But here, impossible. I might as well endeavour
To sharpen wit upon a melon. Only against my peers
Can I show greatness, show my powers of cut and thrust
And crushing disputation, emerge the victor,
Start to map out the dialectic and semantic frontiers
Of my God.

IV

Abelard's Arrival in Paris

Paris! Though all these many years have passed
Nothing dims the memory of that day, extraordinary to me
As no other, for the sense of destiny forever locking
Itself into new tracks, the gates of the past
Banging shut behind me. But what is most woven
Through imagination's warp is this: the slow fall away
Of open spaces, only coppices moving imperceptibly
Around the horizon to mark my progress across the chalky seas
Of Beauce and the Ile de France. Then feeling under me
New rhythms, my donkey stiffening his legs
To brace himself against the dropping levels,
The scramble up and down the river valleys,
And greetings in a different accent rising
From the little vegetable plots where farmers bent

Over carrots, onions, and moved among the dappling apple trees.
How the barns quickened as if themselves in march
And gathering pace towards the city!
On, on, through villages of staring people,
Past covered markets, the blood of freshly slaughtered chickens
In their runnels, the wearying hostels with no good meat
Or wine, and out of the gutters the upheld hands, the crying,
Shouting, wailing, the heat, the stench, my donkey shying
At ghosts and men, the percherons of nobles being led
To stable, the hunting hounds, the gables, the famous churches,
And then the surge, sweet moment sluicing through the city gates,
In over mud and rubbish to break against the river island,
God's beehive, stone fortress walling round the sanctuaries
Of the first martyr, broken by men's stones.

V

Héloise, Ward and Niece of Fulbert, Paris

What should a small girl do under the towers?
I like to walk the long quays that smell of fish,
Play in my uncle's apple orchards a stone's throw
From the city's palaces. The city graves itself
Upon my heart in all its paradoxes, the paradox
Of sex and education, my intellect bending phenomena
To the questions why, what is reality, what it is
To be woman, fidèle, comely, needing to understand God.

Orphaned, I was brought here by my uncle
And very early learned to love the sound of earnestness,
Men's voices rising off the walls and raised a little only
As they are when their world's vision catches in the crack
Of another's. Slowly, by dint of hearing,
The infant mind begins to billow with the wind
Of speculation on that one thing which is everything
And which at all times filled the mouths of those around me: God.

VI

Fulbert, Canon of the Cathedral of St Etienne, Paris

She is my only niece, orphaned, my favourite sister's child,
Hersinde, who dances still in my memory like a dragonfly.
Hersinde was spirit, counsellor, adversary and friend,
Strong forgiver and formidable jouster with words.
All my youth is filled with delight of her
And bitterness at how she was wasted
Upon the banal things men expect of women
And with which most women, unlike her, connive:
Compliance, domesticity, the blunting of the intellect
Upon the dull instruments of everyday.
That she should die in the most commonplace of all
Has been her message to me for her daughter:
I want an education to place Héloise with the best,
Nor any opportunities for death to bundle her into his precincts
Before her time, before she has achieved her proper dignities.
This is why I have procured the most superior in France
So she shall learn to be her own mistress in the eyes of God.

VII

Héloise's Schoolroom

Mine's a tough education, my room
Deliberately set off for me, my own chamber of studies
With the philosophers, orthodox, alchemical,
Academia's and Christendom's, the small mind
Struggling with these new notations to tame them,
Not old enough to grasp in their enormities
The eternal problems, solutions remaining
More elusive than the harmony of spheres.

Here is my work cabinet: step in and walk around.
It will be necessary for you to have familiarised
Yourself with it by and by.
A trunk for clothes, a table, chair and trestle,
Small altar, casket where we put the consecrated bread,

Rushes summer and winter, and one tapestry we roll away
When the spring's fully out. Otherwise, the real companion
Here's the play of light and shadow off the chapter walls,
Dark when I need to work, and full of air and birdsong
When curiosity makes me push wide the window
And watch the men, walking, gesticulating, below.
And this is where I think what will I be?

You ask what of housewifery, midwifery, friends?
For the first two no theory nor practice except the practice
That all households have: I watch how women
Minister daily, gladly or ungladly, for men;
How men minister to themselves or God;
I choose the latter.
No sense, then, of missing the company of girls
Who could not show, nor speak to me, of what's begun
To flourish in me: ceaseless desiring
To find, transfixed in every object, its immortal essence,
To see this essence naked to the eye.

Example: under the beam which overhangs my window
Housemartins nest. Through the seasons, I love them:
First, the inexhaustible diligence of flying up and back,
Up and back, up and back, to build their clay shelters
Like grapes on the vine, yet stronger than fortresses.
Their wings like arrows, the eye encompassing
Instantaneously the element upon whose precipice
They hang to launch themselves. But most of all,
The flight of housemartins is a chiselling of air,
The making of a sky tapestry, the twisting of the seam
Through matter, the unconscious dance of God.

VIII

Abelard in the Mason's Yard

Here in the mason's yard the new and old conjoin.
But conjoin's a strange word to use of stone.
When what you think of is prime matter, the irreducible
Nature of rock chosen precisely to weather out
Mortality and shape our thoughts of heaven in a human space.
And yet the bending of the stone under the mason's hand
Shows us what this coupling means: his imagination's
Now fixed into a medium that's also ours,
Become our property and province within whose frontiers
We can learn to walk and then ourselves may alter
In time the circumferences of our own minds
And out of this create perpetually world upon world,
The image of creation's ceaseless recreation.
Look how he frees from the prison of the stone
These elders of the Apocalypse, making each one a likeness
For us to discover what we really are: he who is curious
To verify his God, and leans out perilously; he who contorts
His whole being passionately to marvel; he who is content
To wait, and, finally, these others, clothed in serenity,
Looking away.

IX

Héloise and Her Teacher, Peter Abelard

This is my work cabinet where he came every day.
The best teacher in the land, the one who most knew
How to show me the way to learning for myself
The skills which he was master of.
This is the generosity of the truly great instructors
Who give so freely of their heart's passion
That, like the flames each lit from one Paschal candle,
The fire leaps out and across and is set up
In all the pupils' hearts. He was not lenient,
Nor brutal; but always in our lessons he would lead
Deeper into the complexities of what we think

And know, and can know, about our inner and our outer worlds.
This I learnt from him: that when you're young,
There is a kind of adequate knowledge that we have,
That youth's an age of certainties, swift intellectual decisions
And enthusiasms that form the bedrock out of which we grow.
But if as we get older there's no movement, question, change,
Then we are lost to understanding, for only in radical mutation
In the way we see can we flourish to full maturity.

X

The Song of Abelard

When the leaf falls
Is the season
I first came to the presence
Of Héloise.

In her high chamber
I taught her, we talked
And the apples ripened
Upon the trees.

We talked, and she taught me
What I had misvalued,
The sleekness of womanhood,
Her intellectual beauty.

Héloise is my lover,
My mistress, my concubine,
My wife and my sister
For all to see.

When the leaf falls
Is the season of Héloise;
Sing her with all your might:
This is what lovers may well be.

XI

Rumour

They do say round the town
Runs a rumour like this:
X copulates with So-and-So
And is in bliss.

In bliss? The bastard So-and-Sos.
What does it mean? We'll try
To bring them down again,
To make them cry.

We'll muscle through their intimacies,
We'll plague their hours in bed,
Make corruption of their sweetnesses,
Kill their love-making dead.

Don't ask me why; it's obvious.
They have what we don't know.
We're envious, and powerful:
Ours is the market show.

XII

Abelard: The Work of Art

What is the purpose of the work of art for God?
It is the philosophical imagining of how creation might exist
Before it happens. Rather as before you travel you may trace
Signs made by others to give you control and balance
And for orientation also, suggestions of the terrain,
Seas to be crossed, notional distances, and yet
Know nothing of, and, moreover, know that nothing
Can be knowable about the realised landscape,
The river meander, the rocky vastness, the streets' configurations,
Until you move like the first being on the first day
Through them and understand that it's in this *particular* form
The first stage of creation coalesces.
This is the certitude from which you depart.

It's certitude because you have arrived at least
At a place where contours are defined, remembered.
The next stage is where the mind may run mad,
Trying to envisage what creation *really* is
The quickening out of this theatre of the apparently immutable
All the existences, experiences, eyes, of all the beings
That have ever been.

They do say in that in the cold caverns of Guyenne
Exists a dragon, or a dragon-like thing:
White skin, whip body and tail, four tiny legs and paws,
Three different ways of breathing, fish, tadpole, human.
These are its modes of living in the utter dark.
A work of art may be this: the attempt to imagine
Into being unthought-of monsters, and, in so doing,
Shoot one more infinitesimal arrow of comprehension
Obliquely between us and the mind of God.

XIII

Bernard of Clairvaux: The World of Sense and the Church

The place of God is not a place for bestiaries.
In what way do a griffon, serpent, lion, enlighten us
Upon His charity? And all the hours spent on the endeavour
To elaborate this cornucopia of deformity
Are hours not spent considering our own unworthiness,
The self-immolation necessary to afford a glimpse
Of nature purged of all that's earth.
For all these are the dragging down of spirituality
Into the farmyard, the common byre and wood
And stream and, worse, into the pit of our imaginations
Where hell lives, monsters, conjurings of experiences
Long extinct, the very raging of our bestial self.
The sanctioning of this cacophony within the church
Is blasphemous, a spinning out of useless forms
For man's amusement and lubricity only,
The glorifying instead of God of fairground tricks
And drunk excesses, of women's open legs
And man's bared, sickening arse.

XIV

The Refectory, The Convent of Sainte-Marie, Argenteuil

That day in the refectory: when you,
Already in retreat away from Paris as we tried to conquer rumour,
And yet unable, as was I, not to meet, not to feast
Upon each other's words and touch; that day,
When, for seclusion, you hustled me
In the silence of the hour for prayer
Through a side door among the trestle tables
And evidence of the community's communion,
Their individual faces, manner, laughter,
Large and familiar in our minds down all the benches;
Yes, in the silence of their ignorance,
I pushed away the veils about the beauty
Of the woman upon earth I most desire,
And you showed me all your succulence and longing
To cradle me between your legs, and did so;
Whether this was not prayer, that day in the refectory,
Dare we say yes or no?

XV

Héloise to Her Son, Astralabe

What were you for us? Your arrival coming untimely,
Unasked-for, containing in it the unimaginable catastrophe,
You were the exemplar of heredity's weight,
The ambiguity of birth, the terror of projection
Into what will come. A legend tells of how the elf-bride
Of man laughs in the village at its deaths, weeps
At its births, and how her husband loses her
For failure to understand; his incomprehension
Makes a mockery of those conventions that pretend
Joy and sorrow at the fate of others,
When all we celebrate and mourn is our desires.
And as to that bride your coming brought me also
Bad dreams, obscure presentiments and fears
Of what it is to give life. We have no notion

59

Really of what it means, yet can be sure the facts
Of pain and anguish, ultimately death, are inescapable.
Nor is even the adult's enlightenment upon these points assured.
Did we inflict life on you? A life which neither
Mother nor father could properly assume?
For you represented the resurgence of all that world
Which is so natural, so infinitely to be hoped for,
Which beckons us indescribably sweetly with its promise
Of a real happiness, the ancient happiness of hearth
And forward geniture, the proof of our ability
To participate in events long after
Our own transformation by death.
But what of now, the fact that we are also this embodiment?
This is what I saw: the place for neither Abelard nor me
Was in the bridge a new human being makes,
For he grows up and into other cities;
And that is right.
But some should set themselves apart to achieve now
What will otherwise never come: the delving down
Into the mysteries of why at all the human personality,
Of why it is indeed a necessary thing for man to know himself,
For without this knowledge comes the waking nightmare
Of calamity for every soul on earth.

XVI

Abelard: of Universals and Particulars

The essence that is in the world is of the world,
No fiction approximating to another place
Where you may snatch eternally at archetypes
Eternally fleeing from the individual mind.
That's endlessly to place ourselves and nature
Beyond the pale of proper scrutiny, to postpone,
In peril of our souls and bodies, that great investigation
Into dread and beauty which is the responsibility
We bear for being real.

That is the flaw: to believe that dread,
The manifestly evil, exists in our material parts alone,
While beauty, goodness, subtend always the mystic,
The place elsewhere. For here's the paradox:
There is no beauty, goodness, that does not know
Its counterpart; unconsciousness of self 's
At best a stale adornment, at worst
The pit of murder and its pleasures.
We cannot inhabit an existence in which we wilfully deny
Our own need to face the irresolvable,
Nor where we court the hasty and too facile answer
And split asunder philosophically those things
It's difficult for our too lazy faculties to reconcile.
And most of all, beware the separation at the heart of things:
In your own being. The truths that are emotion,
Intellect, sensation, faith, and not their *synthesis*,
Are like emperors upon a dusty highway,
Whose vast and glittering palanquins obscure
The assassins waiting at the city gate.

XVII

Fulbert

Rocking, rocking. The window goes back and forth;
The world's got like a pendulum, rocking upon a single thread:
My pain. To think that in this room he used her
As her plaything, played upon my trust and eagerness,
Took out his cock and fucked her – like a whore!
Forget philosophy; he even used her in his grammar lessons
To make his students laugh. So all's a game of logic.
Proposition: that I take away the maidenhead
Of the best of them to see if she's more readily mastered
Than a syllogism. And she was.
That my niece, my cherished niece, who had everything
To lift her up, to destine her for office, influence,
Power, should so disgust me by opening her legs to the firstcomer
And fall pregnant like a goat girl tupped in a stall.

But now, it's worse: the rumour of clandestinity comes,
Even after marriage, even after I worked so hard
To shake dishonour off, to stop the sniggering on corners,
The mutterings in my brain.

But what if he does this deliberately, to run another mockery
Into my face, utter rejection of me, subordination
Of *my*, Fulbert's, family to his own ambition?
Thus he treads across my skull for his preferment. I'm betrayed.
Well, there's a law which says: he who has dishonoured
Shall be ten times dishonoured: he who has inflicted pain
Shall know the mire of pain that never goes away.

At last, the room's grown quiet. I've stopped the pendulum.
All's still.

XVIII

Arnolphus, Notary

By market time, the whole city knew:
How, about four in the morning,
(Because a certain butcher of the quartier
By the name of Robert gave witness later
At the depositions) on his way to matins,
He had heard cloaked figures in a doorway
Discussing entry and what excuse to give;
How, upon rousing Pierre Esbillart, the occupant,
To come and open to an emergency,
The two hired men had first bound his hands,
Produced a knife and stripped him naked,
Then, before raising the alarm, sliced off his genitals.

XIX

Héloise to Abelard

As if shame for your mutilation had destroyed,
Like those men your physical manhood,
This your emotional, you fled me
Into the most disgusting recess of your imagination
And there performed a far more terrible castration:
You took away from me all hope.
You say, what hope, when you're a monster
Among men and must creep from their gaze
As women do, and piss like women do,
And feel your very body changing to a thing
That neither man nor woman recognises;
Yet I should recognise you
If you had not transformed yourself through cowardice.

Not even once into your presence have you let me come,
Though you well know our conversation's the light
Of my existence and your embraces burn
Through my nights and through my flesh like flame.
How will I bear this metamorphosis
Through year upon year of longing, dragging a body
Destined by God to have you, and denied;
How will I turn myself into the withered tree?
You ask me even this: that at the height of womanhood
I should forego not only your mind, love, body,
Sweeter to me than the burning rose,
But all the world as well. You ask me,
'Because you cannot have me', to withdraw
For ever and wall myself into this convent tomb.
Do you once suspect how glacial the air of the cloister
Is to me? How I find no solace whatsoever
In what is nonetheless supposed to offer hope?
So, while these other women round me
Are nourished by a food I cannot see,
My own mind must shrivel and bang itself
Around my cell like a broken bird?

And yet, so much have I wished to be with you,
I'd rather be one in God with you

63

Than lie beyond your circumference.
Not to do what you ask is unimaginable;
You had not even made one step, when I rushed
Before you into the arms of God.

XX

Abelard to Héloise

You say, a coward. Can you conceive of what it is
To lose your manhood? To rage against the walls
Of my sickroom with thinking that never again
Would we lie together, never again
Would I be able to lie in you?
The image of your face first turned towards me,
Full of questions; the way you learned the fierce demolishing
Of logic, and arguments upon the right way in morality;
Your face in ecstasy upon the pillow, burning, burning.

Héloise, there is a circumstance when shame's
So paramount in the soul's private world
It operates a cutting back of all the life
Which went on there before, forcing the spirit
To transform or die. This is the shame
Of being victim, and not the guilt of perpetration
That you might expect. No, this is more subtle by far;
How can I forgive myself for what was done to me?
Should I not have fought, or guessed a motive,
Placed myself differently? In my whole life not been
So sure of honour, so exultant in success?
Slowly, out of the pain and shadows, a problem
More intimate than any other looms:
The irrevocable drops like an axe forever
Upon experience, *ours*, and severs it;
Being truly mutilated, I see that I am merely emblematic
Of the inescapable mutilation life brings.
The differences do not matter
Because our destiny's severance
And our most difficult responsibility
Is to crush it underfoot.

XXI

Abelard, Abbot of the Monks of St Gildas-en-Rhuys, Basse-Bretagne

Out here by the sea I can think. I leave
All those recalcitrant men of God
To stew in their rivalries and inability
To be what they claim to be.
Their mouths reiterate old words for higher things;
Their minds do not. They shuffle, machinate,
Bring down decisions that re-organise power
Away from private interests, do anything
With all their intellects except consecrate
Themselves to understanding.
They do not have the wit to look into their soul
And see that ever more muddied waterhole,
Nor comprehend why all around rises mephitic silence.

These are the men supposed to enlighten others
Concerning evil, guilt, redemption, death;
And yet each morning I see how they're unable
To raise their eyes from petty loyalties,
Complacency, even actions that explicitly deny
The love they stand for. Indeed, how could they?
They're locked within the system of their own spirit,
And long have jettisoned that clarity
Which enables self to burst through the bubble
Of personal reality and see what they profess and cannot do
Under the eye of eternity. If this is true
Of those who are ostensibly invested
With spiritual influence in the affairs of men,
What are we to hope from those who have lost even this,
Who boil in court and law court, family and marketplace,
With now and now and now and now and now?

XXII

Héloise on Marriage

I will never accept that what we did was wrong.
Indeed, both your, and my, misfortunes, stem
From your perceived denial that I was your wife.
And yet wife was the one thing I did not wish to be.
What is marriage but a condemnation of our independences
To domesticity? Imagine it: how could you begin to think
Amongst the chaos that it all would bring?
The morning scene: babies needing to be washed and fed,
Their squalling sicknesses and indispositions,
Servants shouting in the kitchen,
Salesmen knocking at the door,
The very woman that you love so much
Torn into a thousand fragments,
Angry, flustered, resentful.
How you would long for the cool stones of your study,
How I would come to hate you for it,
Shut out forever from the garden of the mind,
Unable to hear, for all the tumult,
The water of our conversations flowing.
You know I'd rather be your concubine for a thousand years
Than wife. Your concubine, exactly that –
The woman who lies with you.
For it's not solitude I want, a turning endlessly
Round the frozen core of myself; I want independence in reciprocity,
The freedom to love you and lie with you as we please,
The intercourse of our minds like bees in a herb garden,
Of our bodies like the dances of dolphins.

XXIII

Abelard: Evil and Sin

Here the question opens, like a chasm
Where the mind's young stallion, who only yesterday
Frolicked over the prairies of logic,
Comes to a standstill.
What is evil? What is sin?
These questions have made monkeys of all the philosophers
And yet the simplest man on earth must face this gap
Between a perfect and an imperfect world;
He fills his prime, but must grow old,
And must watch others die.
Where does it come from? Outside or in?
If from without, responsibility's removed from us
And placed eternally at another's door:
My neighbour's or my enemy's, a quirk of birth, or feeding,
Education, the malice of my competitor,
Incompetence, ignorance, ice-cool indifference,
Or the hot, dry jigglings in the devil's brain.
A reassuring principle, yes; we are the victim,
Carved into our shape by countless evil agencies
That God's allowed to toy with us, before He scoops us up
Like puppets to wash away the marks of hatred
And deck us out for immortality.

Can we accept this? Here all is predeterminate;
We do nothing but undergo erosion like the limestone cliff
And all our consciousnesses are only stupid waiting games
Played by the mad alchemist in his laboratory, God.
And this shows worse, for here you see
How He's become our scapegoat, or, if not Him,
Another, called Everyman. Everyman, that is,
That is not *me*.

⋆　　　⋆　　　⋆　　　⋆

67

Let it go; allow that we're responsible.
For what exactly? Our own actions?
But what should we exclude?
You see the difficulty, for now we start to slide
Dangerously among the categories.
Grant physiology. It makes no sense for us
To order heartbeat, breathing, the colour of our skin,
All morally neutral. The rest is not so easy.

What's to catastrophe? We do not lecture
The surging river or boiling mountain
Upon the ethics of flood or vulcanicity,
And yet we rage over the devastated ground
And people die. Shall we take upon ourselves the burden
Of a hurricane's guilt? We call these acts of God
But they're more properly acts of geology, weather, tide,
The vicissitudes that come with being susceptible to change
Which we call Nature. Though these are evil in their consequences,
They are not what we mean by God, or sin.
Man's concern, of necessity, must be man's evils;
Those that are done by man are not imputable to God.
We are the implicated, not all for every act
Yet all, perhaps, in every act, because each act
Is for the actor, me, and he is human.
So wisdom lies in not rejecting knowledge
Of another person's mind. I say, knowledge,
Not acceptance. Without knowledge
We cannot know whether to accept or censure
Whereas foreclosure on this knowledge dooms us most certainly
To both a personal and public hell.
For hell is this: not the forks nor prongs
Nor unceasing fire; no, it's the forgetfulness
Of what we do when we forget our fellow man
And our denial that such forgetting
Demands supreme forgiveness.
This is the image of it: a naked skeleton,
Clothed with skin, who slowly turns his eyes upon us,
As he crawls on all fours in the dust.

XXIV

Bernard of Clairvaux, Prosecutor of Abelard Before the Council of Sens

You'll not teach faith by questioning
Nor morality by chopping logic on intent;
What's wrong is wrong, wrong because man is fallen
And what exists below can throw off corruption
Only by trust and prayer and weeping tears of loathing
Over just how disgusting our nature really is.
You know this is the case, and nothing man does with his intellect
Is worth a fig against this.
Sirs, this man is dangerous.
He puts before us that an act is neutral
Until we scrutinise the intentions of the perpetrator –
As if adultery, killing, usury, or fornication
Can be tossed as lightly as dandelion seed upon the wind.
A man who would make geometry of his religion
And pick apart the Trinity with a pair of compasses
To show us *understanding* of our faith
Is something like the serpent we uniquely fear.
He tells us ideas are concepts, not substance, mere words
Denoting things we can perceive – what is this but a trick
Of grammar, a conjuror's illusion to make us doubt
That infusion into us which is the supreme being, God?
Look, sirs, upon the kind of life he leads:
A monk without humility or discipline,
A teacher of subversions, prelate without responsibility,
Converser with women; in short, an abbot of misrule.
And worse, if worse is possible, a man who's not a man,
Eunuched for his own sin, for luxuriating in his lust
For women; where will his body be at resurrection?
Is he not literally cut off forever from the gaze of God?

XXV

Abelard to Héloise on the Council of Sens

I promised you an account though it's been long in coming.
I have a terror that they'll break my will,
The will of the great Abelard, the mocker,
The seeker out of fallacies, the dialectician
Who dazzled France. Héloise, my body and spirit are breaking
And yet still I know I am right.
My misfortune is to tell the spirit of the age
What it will not know. Nor dare it treat me
With the disdain of silence, precisely because I have refused
To keep my own. This means proscription, banishment;
I see how savage they have all become
In the assertion of their rectitudes.
Héloise, it was like this – still thinking
I should receive fair hearing, I come into a hall
And see down all the rows of clergy the faces lined into hostility,
A wall of hatred, power-hunger, prejudice.
I tried to speak, but Bernard held the floor
With such tenacity (and I see now, skill),
That they were stamping for my condemnation
And not one sentence of my *Theologia* heard.
The worst indignity: to have to go through this
Smelling the belch of their eating and drinking,
Looking at men slumped sideways on the benches,
Snoring with wine and pure indifference
Except to stumble 'Condemn! Condemn!'
At an orchestrated moment. They had not one idea
Of what they judged, nor wanted to;
The purpose, after all, was not debate, nor proof,
Nor disproof, nor consensus, but to outlaw and eliminate.
Nor, though Bernard's a man the strength of whose convictions
Goes unmatched in Christendom (except perhaps for mine),
Was there here anything other than the hard odour
Of power in doctrine, the towering of orthodoxy over love.
Maybe too strong a tower for me to storm again;
Before, they burned my books, but now more subtly
They devise to make me renounce what I have staked my faith on,
Declare myself anathemata, castrate myself twice.
This is the cleverness of it: the way to break a man's
To make him first accuse, then mutilate, himself.

70

XXVI

Abelard, Hermit and Abbot of the Paraclete, to Héloise

No other person should have this place but you.
When I first came here, rain thrashed across the coppices
Like Furies, moss dripped in all the pools and from the branches,
I found the world turned inward, the very image of my inner self.
Pushed out at lancepoint by God's self-appointed minders,
Removed forever from the solace of union with you,
I needed my lair like a mountain lion
To hide the shame and blood.
A man grown mentally and spiritually thin
Must go back down towards the earth
And listen to the rhythm of grassblade,
Wind, animal run, the pressure in his veins and arteries
That are all hidden by the clutter in his brain.
And in the weeks before I could even hear one piece of birdsong,
I did what I had never done before: used my hands,
Used picks and talked to people from the farmyards,
Gathered sticks and walked the countryside
Until I could recognise each stream, each pathway,
Every household, every distinctive tree
And my prayerhouse was built.

★   ★   ★   ★

Dedicatee, paraclete,
Encourager and advocate,
Comforter, the bearer-up,
The voice of intercession.
These are the reeds,
This is the thatch
I built with my hands
To house you –
Though you have no true home
But my heart.

★   ★   ★   ★

Why choose to pray to this most abstract thing?
The years of thought and meditation here brought this:
There must be fusion. It is man's principle,
It is God's principle, it is the principle of nature.
You say, what fey, block-headed optimism;
The principles of hate, decay, derision
Lie in our very beds. You'll even point out
That I have used logic apparently to undermine
The principle of unity. This is not true,
For Unity is not the same as One.
And palpably the universe denies it, for contemplating
The multiplicity of created things will make you mad.
Next, how can we admit duality?
It may sometimes be useful to talk of light, dark,
Man, woman, air, water, but ultimately this kind of opposite's
A windswept plateau where we force the ambiguous rockshapes
Into our own false geometries.
There is only this left possible:
The image of the abstract and the concrete
Fused, which so produces something which is neither one nor other,
Is itself, but contains both and is separate from them.
Maybe the schoolmen have forgotten it, but not the rest.
We learn it in the loves and copulations of all things,
And in their self-transcendence, the spirit
Which breathes from them, the neglected paraclete.

    ★   ★   ★   ★

This is why no other person could have this place but you.
In this quiet oratory where nothing under noonday but the wood dove
  moves,
And in you, Héloise, I have accepted two things:
That man without God and woman, and woman without God and man,
Is a tetchy beast at best, self-absorbed, mean-spirited,
Melancholic; at worst, beyond the worst of all our imaginings.

XXVII

Peter the Venerable, Abbot of Cluny,
to the Abbess of the Paraclete, Héloise

As a man coming to the walls of a great city
Of which for many years he's read in books,
I write to you now. There's disbelief and wonder
At the look of the real towers and gateways,
The true complexities of the lived life.
You know your husband died with us.
Perhaps reconciled, in his inmost mind,
To what his destiny had been, how it might bind
The intellect more tightly to the only great discussion
There can be, of first and last things.
He served these questions like no other man,
To lay the emphasis on the mind's co-operation
With the Trinity and its unique relation
To the in-spirer, and most mysterious element,
The fire that fosters understanding and whose understanding,
In the title of this monastery, he bequeathed to you.

Sister in Christ, you know better than anyone
The eagle of affliction does not go away;
That's why your ministry's become an emblem of the paraclete;
You are the crag that swallows screams, the sheltering leaves
Of the willow tree, the knowledge of the fierce dove with throat ablaze
That orders us to witness to the resurrection.

Above the door in the abbey church at Vézélay
I placed it all, all that I've learned from you and Abelard.
All joy and sorrow's there, all ambiguities, embraces,
The monstrous forms and hardly to-be-thought thoughts,
The apostles going out like comets through the cheering streets of heaven,
Christ's slow, effortful, miraculous dance through rock and ocean
To arrive simultaneously at the centre of each man's misery
And as the eye which outreaches space.

Until it is your time to meet this mystery,
My sister in Christ, I give you and the nuns of the Paraclete
Abelard's body and, by the authority of my office,
I absolve him from all his sins.

73

ALSO BY HILARY DAVIES

The Shanghai Owner of the Bonsai Shop (1991)

'. . . terrific value . . . each one of its five sections might have been fleshed out into an entire collection by a less confident and imaginative poet . . . her imagination ranges, searching out and transforming experience . . . a storyteller whose narratives are as unusual as they are compact and tightly-written . . . her transformations remind me of Thomas Traherne's vision in *Centuries of Meditation.*'
HELEN DUNMORE, *Poetry Review*

'impeccably cadenced . . . perfectly paced'
MICHAEL HULSE, *Acumen*

'[It would be] hard to imagine contemporary British poetry without the individual and clear voice of Hilary Davies. Her work shows the influences of both American and French verse, and her command of image, as well as her profound feeling for the decorum of a topic, signal her as a voice . . . loud and clear during the 1990s.'
BRUCE MEYER, *Quarry* (Canada)

'a style reminiscent of Elizabeth Bishop'
SEAN O'BRIEN, *Sunday Times*

Other books in the same series include

ANNA ADAMS   *Green Resistance: New and Selected Poems*

SEBASTIAN BARKER   *The Hand in the Well*

FRANCES CORNFORD   *Selected Poems*

KEVIN CROSSLEY-HOLLAND   *The Language of Yes*

KEVIN CROSSLEY-HOLLAND   *Poems from East Anglia*

MARTYN CRUCEFIX   *A Madder Ghost*

DAVID GASCOYNE   *Selected Prose*

DAVID GASCOYNE   *Selected Verse Translations*

PHOEBE HESKETH   *A Box of Silver Birch*

JEREMY HOOKER   *Our Lady of Europe*

JUDITH KAZANTZIS   *Swimming Through the Grand Hotel*

BLAKE MORRISON & PAULA REGO   *Pendle Witches*

VICTOR PASMORE   *The Man Within*

RUTH PITTER   *Collected Poems*

JEREMY REED   *Sweet Sister Lyric*

ANTHONY THWAITE   *Selected Poems 1956-1996*

EDWARD UPWARD   *Christopher Isherwood:
Notes in Remembrance of a Friendship*

EDWARD UPWARD   *The Scenic Railway*

Please contact Enitharmon for a full catalogue of these titles

77